GOD'S
Unfailing
LOVE

DESSIE J. DANTZLER

ISBN 978-1-63844-681-1 (paperback)
ISBN 978-1-63844-682-8 (digital)

Christian Faith Publishing, Inc.
832 Park Avenue
Meadville, PA 16335
www.christianfaithpublishing.com

Printed in the United States of America

God's Unfailing Love

Because of the Lord's Great love we are not
consumed, for his compassions never fail. They are
new every morning; great is your faithfulness.
—Lamentations 3:22–23 (NIV)

Recently, as I pondered the Crucifixion of our Lord and Savior Jesus Christ, it quickly became a time of reflecting on the love of God. We often hear that God loves us as a father. So in relating to a father's love, I recalled that I grew up in a large family where my parents provided for our needs and of course, that was their way of expressing their love for us, but we seldom heard them say, "I love you." Still, we knew that they cared and loved us in unspoken words—through their actions.

I then began to ponder God's love as a Father more deeply. Through prayer and reading of the Word, I was assured over and over again that God loves us unconditionally and he is faithful to his word. Even now, I am reminded that Jesus expressed his love through his action (dying on the cross) and his spoken word.

But God demonstrates his own love for us
in this: While we were still sinners, Christ died
for us. (Romans 5:8 NIV)

The Lord appeared to us in the past, saying:
"I have loved you with an everlasting love; I have

drawn you with loving-kindness. (Jeremiah 31:3 NIV)

As I continued to read and meditate on the words "God loves me," oh, the joy and the love of my heavenly Father flooded my heart. Without a doubt, we can be assured of God's love in good or difficult times because of his unfailing love and compassion that never fails, and they are new every morning.

Prayer

Dear heavenly Father, thank you for parents and guardians who loved us in the best way they knew how. Thank you for your demonstration of your compassion and unfailing love. O Lord, let us not be remiss to take the opportunity to demonstrate real, true, genuine love and compassion to those we are in contact with from day to day. This we ask in Jesus's name. Amen!

When You Look at Jesus, What do You See?

———— ⟋⟍⟍ ————

The woman then left her waterpot, and went her way into
the city, and said to the men, Come, see a man which told
me all things that ever I did: is not this the Christ?
—John 4:28–29 (KJV)

Have you ever looked at different situations of life that have occurred or anything that you didn't quite grasp the real meaning of? There are many twists and turns in life that leave us blindsided, and we can't quite see our way. Just as the woman in John 4:9, she was busy telling Jesus how the Jews had no dealing with the Samaritans. Also in John 4:25 (KJV), she was waiting for the Messiah (Christ) to come, but she did not see Jesus until he revealed himself.

The truth of the matter is, sometimes we need to refocus and ask him to reveal to us the reality of who he really is. When we look at Jesus instead of our human frailties, we will see peace instead of turmoil and fear, love instead of envy, joy instead of sadness, hope instead of hopelessness, healing instead of sickness, mercy and grace instead of punishment, and forgiveness and salvation instead of eternal damnation. When we look at Jesus, we see compassion and love—so much love—because he went to Calvary's cross and died for our sins in our stead. The list could go on and on, but the point is, when we really look at Jesus through the lens of his eyes, in him we see everything we need. Revelation 22:13 (NIV) clearly states, "I am Alpha and Omega, the beginning and the end, the first and last."

Unless we accept from Jesus that which was bought with his blood and that which he died and rose for, we will experience disheartenment and hopelessness in our own sight. Just as in the above scripture, we want to be able to say, "Come see a man," and that man is JESUS. So the question remains: what do you see?

Prayer

Dear heavenly Father, thank you for your son, Jesus. When I look at Jesus, reveal to me the reality of the benefits of his death and resurrection. Help me walk in the freedom and the assurance of a debt that has been paid in full. This I ask in Jesus's name. Amen.

Awesome God

How awesome is the Lord Most High, the great King
over all the earth! He subdued nations under us, peoples
under our feet. He chose our inheritance for us.

—Psalm 47:2–4a (NIV).

What are your thoughts when you think of God's awesomeness? The question is how awesome is the Lord Most High?
I can't describe or explain him, but he is the almighty God who sent
his only son (Jesus) to die on the cross for the whole world so that
we might live in eternity with him if we believe. He chose our inheritance, but we have to choose our eternity. Let's not miss out on what
has already been paid in full.

Our trip to Jerusalem was an awesome one—walking in the
path Jesus walked, standing on the bank of the Sea of Galilee,
stepping in Jordan River, a visit to Bethlehem, and much more,
but there is no comparison to the awesomeness of God. Maybe
you can think of an awesome occasion you have experienced that
you are able to explain or describe, but the Lord, the great King,
is awesome beyond words. My God is awesome he can do what no
other power can do, and there is no other king that reigns over the
whole earth.

Prayer

Dear Lord, awesome ruler, everlasting Father of the universe, I am so in awe at your greatness and lordship that I cannot fathom your awesomeness. Lord, help me to allow you to rule and reign over every aspect of my life. This I ask in Jesus's name. Amen.

Freedom in Forgiveness

─────── ⟡ ───────

For if you forgive men when they sin against you, your
heavenly Father will also forgive you. But if you do not forgive
men their sins, your Father will not forgive your sins.
—Matthew 6:14–15 (NIV)

Maybe you have been offended, hurt, and experienced mental pain. The act of forgiveness is not always easy or it may be something you are not willing to do. It is then that to forgive becomes a choice that will set you free. Don't any longer let your mind be held hostage by the person or persons through rehearsing the hurt and pain. It is only when you choose to forgive that you can live in freedom from the tormentor of unforgiveness. How much easily said than done, but with a willing spirit and the power of the Holy Spirit, the victory is inevitable.

Just as Jesus shows us mercy and forgives us our sins, we must do the same.

Be kind and compassionate to one another,
forgiving each other, just as in Christ God for-
gave you. (Ephesians 4:32 NIV)

Let it go. Just as the songwriter said, "Don't forget that God in heaven answers prayer. He will make a way for you and will lead you safely through. Take your burden (unforgiving spirit) to the Lord and leave it there." Unforgiveness becomes easier only when we take our burden to him in prayer.

Prayer

Dear heavenly Father, thank you for loving and forgiving me. I desire the spirit of forgiveness with the same mercy, love, and compassion as is in you. Help me to be reminded that if I do not forgive, you will not forgive me. I renounce and repent of the spirit of unforgiveness that I may walk in the freedom Jesus bought with his blood. This I ask in Jesus's name. Amen.

The Greatest Family Reunion

After this I looked and there before me
was a great multitude that no one could count,
from every nation, tribe, people and language,
standing before the throne and in front of the Lamb.
—Revelation 7:9a (NIV)

This is the time of year when families and friends gather from far and near in one State for family reunion, which includes family greetings, food, and fun. In order to have a successful reunion, there must be numerous hours, days or even years of planning and preparation. Can you feel the joy and excitement in anticipation of seeing all the families and friends?

Just as we would like all of our family members and friends to attend this earthly reunion, which takes planning and preparation but only last for a few days, how much more should we long to see our family and friends at the heavenly reunion, which lasts for eternity? Whatever it takes, make plans and preparation to invite your family and friends who have not accepted Jesus as Lord and Savior to become part of the family of God. Jesus is inviting everyone to come to him now so that one day we can all attend the greatest reunion ever.

Just imagine when all God's children get together. What a time, what a time! God has planned the greatest family reunion that we can ever imagine, and Jesus has already paid the fare so that we can be in that great multitude.

Prayer

Dear heavenly Father, thank you for making it possible that everyone can attend the greatest family reunion ever through our Lord and Savior, Jesus Christ. Help us to get busy planning with excitement how we may invite others to you to that family reunion. This we ask in Jesus's name. Amen.

God Is Listening

This is the confidence we have in approaching God: that
if we ask anything according to his will, he hears us.

—1 John 5:14 (NIV)

Do we really know what it means to listen? Of course, we do, but do we really listen? According to *Webster*, "to listen means to make a conscious effort to hear, attend closely so as to hear." I am guilty of not listening all the time when others are speaking directly or indirectly to me. I hear them, but I am not closely listening. Perhaps there has been a time when you needed a listening ear—you called a friend, spouse or even your pastor—and it was just not an opportune time. How frustrating was that?

HALLELUJAH! The good thing is that God is always listening. If we align our prayers to his will, we can be confident that he hears us. We can all call him, anytime and anywhere, at the same time, it is never an inopportune time and nor is there any confusion or mix up. What an awesome God? He may not answer when and how we want him to, but he is listening.

First Peter 3:12a (NIV) states, "For the eyes of the Lord are on the righteous and his ears are attentive to their prayer." So take courage in knowing that he's always attentive to your call, and that whatever the answer, it is always for your good and betterment. Just as this song says, "Now let us have a little talk with Jesus. Let us tell him all about our troubles. He will hear our faintest cry and he will answer by and by."

Consider this: when we send a text massage, we are expecting an answer. So let us expect no less from God because he is greater than all we can think or ask. He has sent the text (the Bible). Expect an answer. He is listening.

Prayer

Dear heavenly Father, awesome ruler, creator and maker of the universe, thank you for you are listening closely to every call and cry. In the name of Jesus, help me to always be aware of your presence and also aware that your ear is attentive to hear the call. Help me to continuously read the text to build my confidence in the knowledge that you are listening and will answer. I ask in the name of Jesus, amen.

Be Still

Be still and know that I am God: I will be exalted among
the heathen, and I will be exalted in the earth.
—Psalm 46:10 (KJV)

How often are we too busy to take the time and know that God
is God and instead start our day or business without consulting him? Nowadays, because of the society we live in, we seldom
have time to be still. We make our television, cell phones, laptops,
and home computers our constant companion. We are comfortable
with having everything done instantly in a microwave style. Even our
churches are too busy being busy with meetings and programs. God
declares in the scripture that he will be exalted. Let us be mindful to
take time out and be still and listen and exalt the Lord.

We see and hear from all over the world of turmoil and disasters, one after the other. Maybe God is trying to get our attention as
he did with Elijah so that He might speak in a gentle whisper (1 King
19:11–12 NIV).

Are you listening for God? Step back from the noise and activity of your busy schedule and be still. He just might be whispering.
Just as the song goes, "Hush, hush somebody calling my name. Oh
my Lord, what shall I do?" In our stillness, he will reveal great and
mighty things.

Prayer

Dear heavenly Father, I come in the name of your only son, Jesus. Thank you being the sovereign and all-powerful God. Thank you for speaking in ways that we can hear you. Help us not to miss you by thinking you only come or speak to us in some great tumultuous, loud, and powerful way when you might come with that powerful gentle voice that can only be heard when we are still. Help us to purposely take time out and be still and know that you are God and that you will be exalted at your appointed time. This I ask in Jesus's name. Amen.

Just Believe God

❦

I will make you a great nation and I will bless you; I will
make your name great, and you will be a blessing.
—Genesis 12:2 (NIV)

What a promise! Abram was a little apprehensive about how
God's promise would come to pass, seeing that he had no
heir to inherit the promise. And "Abram believed the Lord, and he
credited it to him for righteousness" (Genesis 15:5–6 NIV). God
made a covenant with Abram, and he was faithful just as he promised.

Likewise, we are God's children, and we have the privilege
to just believe and take God at his word. Indeed, life is filled with
swift transitions, adversities, and day-to-day challenges. God has not
promised exemption from adversities, but he has promised in his
word he would never leave or forsake us (Hebrews 13:5 NIV). We,
then, must always remember to just believe God and trust Him in
every walk of life.

Therefore, when life throws a curve to knock you off focus,
whether the situation or adversity challenges your health, finances,
offspring(s), or spouse, loss of loved one, job or home, maintain your
course and just believe God. Believing God is a continuous process,
and it is imperative that we trust and totally rely upon him. He is
dependable and trustworthy.

Prayer

Father, in the name of Jesus Christ, thank you for your faithfulness. Help us to believe and trust your promises with our innermost being. We thank you for forgiving our unbelief and accepting our belief that you are faithful just as you promised. This I ask Jesus's name. Amen.

The Truth

To the Jews who had believed him, Jesus said, "If you hold
to my teaching, you are really my disciples. Then you
will know the truth, and the truth will set you free.
— John 8: 31–32 (NIV)

According to *Webster*, there are several definitions for the word
truth, but the one of choice is that the truth is "a particular
belief or teaching regarded by the speaker as the true one." The KJV
dictionary defines the truth as the "conformity to fact or reality; exact
accordance with that which is, or has been, or shall be." I concur
with the scripture and definition that the truth is your freedom. It
brings light to darkness, dispels assumptions, and it frees you from
the bondage of many things that are holding you or have held you
back.

The truth cannot lie because it is the truth; and a lie cannot
speak truth because it is a lie. So it is clear that everything that is not
the truth is a lie. The truth leads you to nothing but the truth because
it knows only the truth. The truth doesn't have any hiding places
because it wants you to know the truth because the truth will set you
free. The truth is your friend and will never tell you anything but
the truth. Some of us may be looking for the truth in many places,
individuals or material things, but the real and sustaining truth to
freedom can be found only in Jesus and his word. If you want to be
free and if you feel you are already free and want to remain liberated,
hold on to the *truth*, which is the Word.

Prayer

Dear heavenly Father, in the name of your only begotten Son, I say thank you for the truth and for being the one who cannot lie. Lord, in our humanness, it is natural for us to look for the truth in something else other than you, but, dear Lord, help us see and know that the Truth is nothing but the Truth, and it will set you free. This I ask in Jesus's name. Amen.

Mountains in Life

Truly I tell you, if anyone says to this mountain, "Go throw yourself into the sea," and does not doubt in their heart but believes that what they say will happen, it will be done for them.

—Mark 11:23 (NIV)

Recently, we were traveling through the mountains to Lake Tahoe. Along the path, I observed many mountains of different magnitude. There were no straight paths but many shallow and deep curves along with the up and down slopes. As we traveled over, around, and through the mountains and through the snow, there were road signs with instructions along the path to help us navigate safely.

So it is with many of our lives. We are faced with different kinds of mountains, curves as well as high and low slopes. In order to navigate through life's difficulties, we are challenged to read and obey the instructions (the Bible) and have faith in the instructor (Almighty God). There is a path over, around or through every mountain that we face regardless of the magnitude. In the process, let us focus on Joshua 1:9 (NIV):

> Have I not commanded you? Be strong and courageous. Do not be terrified; do not be discouraged, for the Lord your God will be with you wherever you go.

Jesus's message is the same to us today: Do not be discouraged. Speak to your mountains because whatever the magnitude of your mountain, he is always present to instruct you along the path. Have faith in God.

Prayer

Our Father, most gracious Master, thank you for being omnipresent. There is no mountain high enough to keep you from your children. Lord, I commit every mountain situation into your hands. Help me to navigate through the mountains in my life according to the instructions you have given me in his word. This I ask in Jesus's name. Amen!

Amazing Love

A new command I give you: Love one another. As I have
loved you, so you must love one another. By this everyone will
know that you are my disciples, if you love one another.
—John 13:34–35 (NIV)

E very day is a chance to show love. There is much talk and acts
of kindness to and for someone we love or even to someone we
don't know, which is great and the right thing to do. So just imagine the greater and amazing love of God. Amazing love is an agape
love—the highest form of love, especially brotherly love, charity, the
love of God for man and of man for God. It is a godly love without
boundaries and/or conditions. God's love for us is so amazing he sent
his only begotten Son to die for us. How much more amazing can
love be when it is until death?

> Greater love has no one than this: to lay
> down one's life for one's friend. (John 15:13 NIV)

Can you see yourself sharing amazing love with someone who
has been mean, unkind, and disrespectful? God did. Today let us seek
out that person whom we think we cannot love for whatever reasons
there may be and share with them God's amazing agape love. This
love is not about how you feel but what is commanded in the above
scripture. Something to ponder: "Love is an unconditional commit-
ment to an imperfect person."

Prayer

Dear Father, thank you for your amazing love, which I cannot fathom. Help me to know this love that is the greatest of all we do on the Christian journey. Help me to find that one person that I may share your amazing agape love with this day. This I ask in Jesus's name. Amen.

A Prayer for Caregivers

O Lord, our God, thank you for being a loving and caring Father. Thank you for new mercies every morning. Thank you for being the source and the strength of our being. Thank you, Father, for when we feel discouraged, we can cry out to you our hope.

Thank you for those individuals who demonstrate your love and compassion by choosing or accepting the task as a care giver. Hide them in your secret place where no evil can harm them as they pour your love and compassion on others. Father, may your grace and mercy abound as they continue to be the hands and feet to those individuals who are unable to care for themselves.

Lord, you never said the task would be easy, but you promise power and strength. Let it be unto every care giver as stated in Isaiah 40:29 (KJV), "He giveth power to the faint and to them that have no might he increaseth strength." So, Lord, I ask for strength for those persons whose pace is constant throughout the day and for the ones who did not sleep last night because someone needed their undivided attention. Lord, have mercy and don't let one become weary in well doing. Grant them the peace of the day through trusting and relying on you because you are the rock in a weary land and a shelter in the time of storm.

Now, Lord, in the midst of all to be done, grant them wisdom and knowledge in how to take care of themselves as they take care of others. Let them continue to be the blessing to others as you are to them. This I ask in Jesus's name. Amen!

God Knows Your Name

For you created my inmost being; you knit
me together in my mother's womb.

—Psalm 139:13 (NIV)

The good news of the above scripture makes it clear that God knows my (your) name. It should give you great comfort and strength knowing that a Holy and Righteous God knows my (your) name among many. Before anyone knew of our being, he knew. So take courage in every case or situation because God knows every detail of your life.

> Lift your eyes and look to the heavens: Who created all these? He who brings out the starry host one by one, and calls them each by name. Because of his great power and mighty strength, not one of them is missing. (Isaiah 40:26 NIV)

I feel confident in saying that if God didn't miss one star, then he is not missing one name of his children. We are truly blessed to know a God that keeps his eyes on everyone at the same time protecting, loving, and guiding us. He knows us *completely*.

Prayer

Dear heavenly Father, maker of heaven and earth, how great thou art. Thank you for your greatness and goodness. Thank you for your handy work in creating each of us uniquely. Thank you for knowing our names and never confusing one with another. Help us to never worry or doubt because you know all the details of our lives. They are bare before you, nothing hidden or missing. Help us ever to be mindful of the only God that loves us and knows our name. This I ask in Jesus's name. Amen.

God's Gift

For God so loved the world that he gave
his one and only Son, that whoever believes in
him shall not perish but have eternal life.

—John 3:16 (NIV)

Christmas comes every year, a time of giving and receiving. Many of us will receive gifts in small or large packages in beautiful wrappings and bows. We will find ourselves anxious and eager to see what is beneath the wrapping. It could be something that you needed or just something that you wanted. It could be something that will last for a few minutes or a lifetime but not eternal.

God gave us a gift that exceeds all gifts—the gift of salvation and eternal life. Because of his love for mankind, he gave his one and only Son (Jesus). He was wrapped in swaddling clothes. His wrapping was not-so beautiful as we know gift wrapping, but beneath the wrapping was the most precious gift given of all time to whoever believes. This gift is absolutely what we need to live a loving, meaningful, and fulfilled life. To one lost soul, give the gift of Jesus, the one who gives the gift of eternal life.

Prayer

Dear heavenly Father, help us to continue to be anxious and eager about the most precious gift given whereby we shall have eternal life. Lord, propel us to share Jesus with the lost and to daily commune with him through reading the Word and fervent prayer. This I ask in Jesus's name. Amen.

Prayer for Healing

Most merciful and gracious Father, I come in the name of Jesus, the one who bore the sins and cares for the whole world on his shoulder. I thank you for being the only true and wise God. Thank you for sending your son, Jesus, to rescue us from the hands and power of the evil one. You are the rock, which holds our anchor, and you are the Balm in Gilead. Lord, I lift up to you the pandemic, COVID-19, over which we have no control. So many are burdened, sick, hurting, and dying from this virus all over the world. Father, hear the cries of your people and send your healing according to Psalm 107:19–20 (NIV):

> Then they cry unto the Lord in their trouble, and he saved them out of their distresses. He sent his word and healed them and delivered them from their destruction.

Father, help us to proclaim the Word just as David did in Psalm 103:2–3 (KJV):

> Bless the Lord, O my soul, and forget not all his benefits: Who forgiveth all thine iniquities; who healeth all thy diseases.

Lord, you are victorious over this virus, and if there be any doubt, replace it with confidence in your Word. Father, there is no disease, situation, or circumstance that's bigger than you. Help us to fix our mind on what we hear in your Word and not on what we see. Lord, thank you for in times of trouble and struggles, you invite us to come to you and find rest. Matthew 11:28 (KJV) says, "Come unto me, all ye that labour and are heavy laden and I will give you rest."

Father, after all is said, help us to realize that there is something required of us. Help us to continue to humble ourselves, pray, and seek your face. Holy Spirit, our leader and our guide, lead and guide those that are in authority and in research of a treatment and cure for this virus.

Father, allow your presence and supernatural power and love to reach deep into our being and then save, protect, comfort, deliver, restore, and heal us. I pray, Lord, let us find solace in knowing that you love us, want the best for us, and that there is nothing hidden from you. Now, Lord, stretch out your hand to perform miraculous signs and wonders through this season. This we ask in the name of your holy servant, Jesus. Amen.

Hope in a Hopeless Situation

———— ✍ ————

To you, O Lord, I lift up my soul; in you I trust,
O my God. Do not let me be put to shame, nor
let my enemies triumph over me. No one whose
hope is in you will ever be put to shame.

—Psalm 25:1–3a (NIV)

Hopelessness presents itself in a horrific and overwhelming way when there is a loss of jobs, homes, finances, death of our love ones, molested children, separation of family, and many other situations in the lives of our families, our friends or our communities. Desperate individuals sometimes seek desperate measures, and unfortunately, there are others whose definition of hope is having money, success, and prestige but still find no inner peace and rest through such gains.

We are living in a highly technological period where a large number of our Christian population are so impersonal and detached from direct human touch that they cannot feel the cares and see the pain in the face of others. Our means of communications lack the hand that reaches out and touches another, that pat on the back or just a smile on someone's face. I'm reminded of the words of this song, "Sometimes you have to encourage yourself. Sometimes you have to speak victory during the test. And no matter how you feel, speak the word and you will be healed. Speak over yourself, encourage yourself in the Lord."

Isaiah 40:31 (NIV) offers additionally encouragement:

> But those who hope in the Lord will renew
> their strength. They will soar on wings like eagles;
> they will run and not grow weary, they will walk
> and not faint.

So in times like these, we have an anchor. His name is JESUS. Be encouraged and do as the psalmist. Put your trust and hope in the Lord Almighty and not in things that cannot sustain.

Prayer

Dear heavenly Father, in the name of Jesus, thank you for being our Lord and Savior. In you, there is hope, complete safety, and security. To you, O Lord, I lift up every soul that feels that they are in an overwhelming hopeless situation. Lord, calm our doubts and fears and let us never despair and lose hope in Jesus, the one who gives us hope. Hear my prayer, O Lord. Amen.

Hindering God's Promises

Therefore I tell you,
whatever you ask for in prayer, believe that you
have received it, and it will be yours.
—Mark 11:24 (NIV)

A couple of months ago, we were encouraged to keep our eyes on the promise keeper, and we were likewise encouraged to remember that all of his promises are true and irreversible. However, sometimes our expectation is not fulfilled. And it is when we do not receive what we are expecting that we begin to rationalize why or we may even doubt whether God really keeps his promises. But surely he does. He is a true and faithful Savior. The above scripture assures us that he is the promise keeper.

We find many promises in the Bible, but a most authentic example of God keeping his promise is that he promised us a Savior (Jesus) for the remission of our sins and the sins of the world. We don't ever have to doubt him because he is the only one in whom we can put all our trust in. He loves us and wants the best for us. God does not keep his promises from us for punishment or just because he can.

But can God's promises be hindered? It is possible that some things pose a hindrance or block to what has been promised such as disobedience, impatience, lack of faith, wavering faith, not listening to God, not knowing what the promises are, and being out of God's will.

James 1:6–7 (NIV) says, "But when he asks, he must believe and not doubt, because he who doubts is like a wave of the sea, blown and tossed by the wind. That man should not think he will receive anything from the Lord." But the good news is if we keep our eyes on the promise keeper, he can help us overcome *anything* that might be hindering his promises.

Prayer

Dear Father, in the name of our Lord and Savior Jesus Christ, thank you for your faithfulness in all your promises that are in your word. I ask your forgiveness for being a hindrance in any way to your promises and blessings. Lord, help me to trust and never doubt that you will do what you said you would do. Amen, amen.

Let God be God

I am Alpha and Omega,
the beginning and the ending, saith the Lord,
which is, and which was, and which is to come,
the Almighty.

—Revelation 1:8 (KJV)

C hallenges and conflict are unavoidable, and these are times to pause and think of all the blessings and benefits of letting God be God in all areas of our lives, because "for the Lord is good and his love endures forever; his faithfulness continues through all generations" (Psalm 100:5 NIV).

Sometimes we think we can handle life's affairs on our own, do it our way in our own timing or however we choose, but there is no other way more effective than God's way. "Thy way, O Lord, not mine; Thy will be done, not, mine. Incline my heart each day to say: Thy will be done" ("Thy Will Be Done").

God is still beckoning his people to let him be God (Psalm 46:10 KJV). We cannot afford to not let God be God, because only He is holy, almighty, righteous, pure, all-knowing, all-powerful, and all-wise. We should let God be God in our lives because he is the only *one* that can do any and everything at the same time. He is the Alpha and Omega, the beginning and the ending. So let him be: Jehovah-Rophe, our healer; Jehovah-Jireh, our provider; Jehovah-Shalom, our peace; Jehovah-Tsidkenu, our righteousness; Jehovah-Rohi, our shepherd; Jehovah-M'kaddesh, the Lord who sanctifies;

and Jehovah-Nissi, our victory. Indeed, God is God, but he will not force himself into our business. But when he is invited in and is made welcome, he is willing and ready to aid us. God is faithful and trustworthy in all his doings.

Prayer

Dear Almighty Father, thank you, the self-existent one who reveals himself in so many ways. Lord, you know what is best for me and you know the way. Help me to let you be God and to let you have control over everything that concerns me. This I ask in Jesus's name. Amen.

Benefits of Loving God

However, as it is written:
"No eye has seen, no ear heard, no mind has conceived
what God has prepared for those who love him."
—1 Corinthians 2: 9 (NIV)

God has prepared something so great and grand for us that naturally we cannot envision or perceive it directly with our intellect. But according to 1 Corinthians 2:10 (NIV), "But God has revealed it to us by his Spirit." When we limit God by our own limitation, still it is hard to receive the revelation of what God has prepared or it could be that sometimes we cheat on God by not loving him wholeheartedly. The condition to receiving the benefits of what God has prepared is to "those who love him." Take a moment, think, and meditate on taking your love for God to the extreme and rely on the Holy Spirit to reveal what God has prepared.

If your relationship and revelation is not clear, one might be asking, *What has God revealed?* The most important benefit God has revealed is that through trusting in Jesus Christ, his only Son, we can have salvation and eternal life. Also, in this life, we can enjoy the benefits of loving God if we are willing and obedient to follow Christ. He has a multitude of blessings in store for us that we have not yet seen, heard, or conceived. John 10:10b (NIV) says, "I have come that they may have life, and have it to the full."

Prayer

Dear heavenly Father, awesome ruler and creator, in the name of Jesus, we laud and exalt your name for you are the Almighty God. Thank you that loving you is never null and void. Thank you for the many, many blessings you have prepared for those who love you. Help me to be mindful not to cheat on you by loving something or somebody more than I love you and not loving you with my whole heart.

This I ask in Jesus's name. Amen!

Where Is Your Faith?

Have faith in God.

—Mark 11:22 (NIV)

Have you ever prayed and prayed again about a particular situation or problem and the answer you were expecting didn't happen? Did you wonder why God didn't answer your prayer? Maybe it was not God's timing or even his will, but still, the above scripture admonishes us to "have faith in God." Also, there are some other conditions that must be met. The scripture said to "say to this mountain." We just can't think it or imagine it, we have to say it, believe, and doubt not it (Mark 11: 23–24 NIV). There is power in the tongue (Proverbs 18:21 NIV).

God is sovereign, holy, and righteous, and all his promises are reliable. He is letting us know by referring to the mountain, that there is no impossible task; he can do anything. Whatever God does, it is always best for us. God loves us, and it is his desire to bless us in every way. And he gets no pleasure from our unanswered prayers. Don't be weary or dismays. "Have faith in God."

Prayer

Dear heavenly Father, thank you for your love and the desire to bless me. Thank you for you are faithful and trustworthy. I ask you in the name of Jesus to never let me doubt my faith in you and the power of your words that I speak. Help me to know the depth of the life in your Word and that it can bring life to any dead situation. I ask this in the majestic name of the risen Savior, Jesus Christ. Amen!

Loving God

But as it is written, Eye hath not seen,
nor ear heard, neither have entered into
the heart of man, the things which God hath
prepared for them that love him.
—1 Corinthians 2:9 (KJV)

It's a wonderful privilege to serve and worship a loving God, the one and only wise God who owes us nothing, but he is ever willing and ready to give us all things. Because of our finite minds, we cannot fathom what God has in store for those who love him. In that his love is so great toward us, loving him should be our foremost and highest priority—first, because of who he is, and secondly, because we are recipients of his most precious gift of salvation, and thirdly, because of the many blessings of his grace and mercy and unconditional love.

Isaiah 64:4 (NIV) also states, "Since ancient times no one has heard, no ear has perceived, no eye has seen any God besides you, who acts on behalf of those who wait for him." God's love and blessings are inexhaustible. What a mighty God he is! Let us take time out daily and ponder our love for God and then strive always to love him with passion as he loves us.

Prayer

Our Father, thank you for all you have prepared for the ones who love you. Help us to continually search for ways to love you more just because of who you are. We want to be a prepared people for a prepared blessing. This we ask in Jesus's name. Amen.

God's Greatness

How great you are O Sovereign Lord!
There is no one like you, and there is no God but
you, as we have heard with our own ears.
—2 Samuel 7:22 (NIV)

We know and have read about many great individuals. We are amazed and awed by their interventions, inventions, and accomplishments for it is fitting for us to give them their accolades and props. So how much more ought we to give our Sovereign Lord praises for his greatness? When I think about the greatness of mankind, it is hard to fathom and see the big picture of God's greatness for his greatness is so advanced. How awesome is this? God is the creator, Lord, and ruler of the Universe. He is the only one who is omnipresent (present in all places at the same time), omniscient (knowing all things), and omnipotent (all-powerful). There is no one to compare.

Listen to the words of this song:

> I climbed up to the highest mountain, I looked all around, couldn't find nobody. Went down into the deepest valley, looked all around down there, couldn't find nobody. I went across the deep blue sea, couldn't find one to compare to your grace, your love, your mercy. Nobody greater, nobody greater than you.

In all of God's greatness, he is still concerned about all of our affairs. He doesn't want us to think, even for one moment, that he is challenged because we think that the smallest concern is too small and that the largest is too large. Acknowledge God in all that you do because it is a true blessing to know a God who is so great yet so compassionate and loving that he is concerned about every detail of our lives.

Prayer

Dear God, our great and mighty master, for your greatness is higher above anything that we can think or imagine. We thank you for allowing us to be a part of your great family and all your greatness. Help us, Lord, not to contain you in our own box of your greatness but explore your greatness through prayer and the reading of your Word. This we ask in Jesus's name. Amen.

The Secret Place

He that dwelleth in the secret place of the
Most High shall abide under the shadow of the
Almighty. I will Say of the Lord, He is my refuge
and my fortress: my God: in him will I trust.

—Psalm 91:1–2 (KJV)

Perhaps at one point in our lives, there was a time when we found comfort, peace, and safety in tangible or perceptible ways. Maybe as a child, it was your parents, your imaginary space, your special toy, or a particular hideout. As an adult, it was your friends, spouse, or a particular habit. In any case, that was your secret place. Think about how you felt.

Now just think about the Most High God, your spiritual secret place. Do you feel that comfort and blissfulness? In all that we see and hear that's going on around us and throughout the world, God is encouraging us through his Word to keep the faith and do not panic. Don't let pain or fear freeze you in place or time. Run to the secret place of the Most High (our Lord and Savior Jesus Christ). He is our shelter and refuge. Even in the midst of all the drama, through it all, we can find safety and security in the secret place of the Most High. He did not promise us that trouble would not come, but he did promise he would always be present (Psalm 139:7–12 KJV).

Trust him, he is a faithful God.

Prayer

Father, I come in the name of Jesus Christ, the loving and ever-lasting one. Thank you for being who you are: a refugee, a rock, a shelter, a resting place, the Savior, and so much more. You are an awesome God. There is no one else who can fill all our needs and concerns so that we can feel totally safe and secure. Lord, where there is unrest and insecurity, replace it with faith and trust. I ask your continuous covering in the secret place under the shadow of which you are the Almighty one. Amen! Amen!

Send Me

(Prayer)

Dear Heavenly Father, thank you for being so gracious and merciful toward us. During the Southern California Annual Missionary Convention, I heard the shout of the words of Isaiah, "Here am I, send me." So I offer this prayer in that many may be willing but don't know where to go, what to do or how to do it. Lord, give clear directions to the ones who are willing but don't know where to go. Father, please calm the fears of the ones who are ready to go but are fearful of going. Give clarity to those who are halted between opinions as to where to go. Lord, help us to be obedient even in the midst of not knowing every detail and to always keep our eyes on you, the one who knows the way.

Father, for those who are clear about where they are being sent and the path they are about to take, I ask that you keep them in your care and cover them with your blood. I pray that they may be assured according to your word that you will never leave or forsake them. Father, help us to trust you with all our concerns and decisions. I ask your guidance and leadership in the path you have already prepared for you know the plans you have for each of us. This I ask in the name of Jesus. Amen.

Trusting God's Word

So shall my word be that goeth forth out of my mouth: it shall
not return unto me void, but it shall accomplish that which
I please, and shall prosper in the thing whereto I sent it.

—Isaiah 55:11 (KJV)

Being human, we sometimes promise some things that we cannot
make it happen, not because we don't plan to be true to our
word but because other things just happen. This is not so with God's
Word. All of *his* words are sure and irreversible. As I was driving one
day, I remember reading these words: "This is God's Word, and it is
true, and it can be trusted." Look at the scripture above, which says
his word shall not return to him void. He is just waiting on us to
trust him wholeheartedly. Is there anything that you would like for
God's Word to accomplish? According to Hebrew 4:12 (NIV), "For
the word of God is quick, and powerful, and sharper than any two
edged sword, piercing even to the dividing asunder of soul and spirit,
and of the joints and marrow, and is a discerner of the thoughts and
intents of the heart." What a miracle-working Word!

God wants us to rest in his promises and to have confident in
his word. Some of the prerequisites to being able to rest in that place
with him are: a relationship with him, surrendered spirit, reader of
the word, willing to obey and trust him; and then you will be able to
walk and live in victory in the word.

Prayer

Most gracious Father, thank you for your word and for making it available to us. Forgive me for not always obeying and trusting you completely. Open my heart and mind to fully understand and comprehend your word and to place full confidence in it. Lord, grant me the will to surrender myself and everything that concern me to you every day so that I will walk in victory. I ask this in Jesus's name. Amen.

Stand on the Promises of God

Your Kingdom is an everlasting kingdom,
and your dominion endures through all generations
The Lord is faithful to all his promises and
loving toward all he has made.
—Psalm 145:13 (NIV)

What do you do when you don't know what to do. I'm sure many of us have heard this as a sermon or just a question thrown out from time to time. Are there times when you have many thoughts about what to do with a particular problem or situation? Being that it could be a diagnosis of bad news about your health, the children or the grandchildren, and/or a financial dilemma or whatever the case may be, but you still don't know what to do. Have you ever continued to ponder, pray, and even consulted an advisor whom you trusted the most, but your decision is still unclear?

So in the midst of your spiraling mind and mixed emotions, here is something you can do: You can ALWAYS stand on the promises of God, the solid and sure foundation that will never give way (the word of God). The above scripture states: "The Lord is faithful to all his promises." And also Hebrew 10:23 (NIV) says, "Let us hold unswervingly to the hope we profess, for he who promised is faithful."

We must hold on to our faith to trust God more. Now let the words of this hymn speak to your heart:

> Standing on the promises that cannot fail, when the howling storms of doubt and fear assail, by the Living Word of God I shall prevail, standing on the promises of God. Standing, standing, standing on the promises of God my Savior, standing, standing, I'm standing on the promises of God.

Pick God's promise and stand.

Prayer

Dear Heavenly Father, thank you for you are a promise keeper. Thank you for I don't ever have to worry about you being true to your word because you are a faithful and loving God. Help us to strive to be just as faithful in trusting you as you are with keeping your promises. We know we can never equal up to your generosity but help us to reflect it. This I ask in Jesus's name. Amen.

The Key-Prayer

Then you will call upon me and come and
pray to me, and I will listen to you. You will seek me
and find me when you seek me with all your heart.
—Jeremiah 29:12-13 (NIV)

P rayer is the key to the kingdom. Have you ever misplaced the
key to a particular door or any lock of importance? At that point,
you tried whatever means were necessary to open the lock. Perhaps
you called a friend or neighbor, but all to no avail. Do you remember
how hopeless you felt? Then you realized you needed to call the one
who knew how to open the lock—the locksmith. What an effortless
job when you called the right person.

Have you thought about the displacement of priorities, the difficulties the world, and even the church are experiencing this day and
time? Maybe we have tried all the avenues we know except *wholeheartedly* call the one who knows how to unlock all difficulties, hard-
ships or distresses that we are experiencing. His name is Jesus.

Let's try Psalm 55:16–17 (NIV):

But I call to God, and the Lord saves me.
Evening, morning, and noon I cry out in distress
and he hears my voice.

Just as the psalmist cried out to God and he heard him, let us
cry out. As Jeremiah did in the above scripture, he is still admonish-

ing us to call, pray, and seek him with our whole heart to unlock the door of every challenge and difficulty. He still hears.

Prayer

Dear heavenly Father, the maker of the universe, thank you. You are the one who knows and can do all things. I call upon you now to unlock the door to our hearts so that we may truly seek you with all our heart. Lord, I ask that we not waste time searching for that which is misplaced but call to you, the right One to unlock the locks of all of the world's challenges and difficulties we are facing right now. Thank you, Lord. This I ask in Jesus's name. Amen, amen.

Trusting God Without Limits

Trust in the LORD with all your heart and lean
not on your own understanding.

—Proverbs 3:5 (NIV)

Whenever it comes to trusting God for what we need or want, we sometime exalt our own self-sufficiency. We tell God what we want and then tell him when and how things should go in order that everything works out as we planned. The truth is God does not need your input or assistance for he knows the plans he has for you (Jeremiah 29:11). Yield yourself to the Holy Spirit and the power of the Almighty God who is capable and able to handle all your cares and needs for he is all powerful (omnipotent), present in all places at the same time (omnipresent), and knowing all things (omniscient). Praise God for who he is. Hallelujah!

When we take the limits of God as we journey through this Christian path, which he has already prepared, then we will see more clearly, and our ears and heart will be open to the things of God. Psalm 37:5–6 (NIV) states:

> Commit your way to the LORD; trust in him
> and he will do this: He will make your righteous
> reward shine like the dawn, the justice of you
> cause like the noonday sun.

God's ability far exceeds anything that we can ask or think. Let go, obey, and trust God.

Prayer

Dear heavenly Father, thank you for never giving up on me in times of doubt and fear. I have no reason to doubt you. You are a faithful God. Help me to place full confidence in you and to trust you without limits. This I ask in Jesus's name. Amen.

What about Love?

Dear friends, let us love one another,
for love comes from God. Everyone who loves has
been born of God and knows God, whoever does not
love does not know God, because God is love.
                                                —1 John 4:7–8. (NIV)

We find ourselves all through the years expressing love in various ways to the special individuals in our lives. We can see from the scripture that to love is to know God. So what about love?

Love is a four-letter word with a strong meaning, which reflects our choices and actions. It is the basis for living a peaceful and fulfilled life. It is unconditional and immeasurable, that strong cord that cannot be broken. It is the tie that binds. It is the sharing and reaching out of oneself. So don't get caught up in the moment of your emotions. According to 1 Corinthians 13: 4–8a (NIV), "Love is patient, love is kind. It does not envy, it does not boast, it is not proud. It is not self-seeking, it is not easily angered, it keeps no record of wrongs. Love does not delight in evil but rejoices with the truth. It always protects, always trusts, always hopes, always preserves. Love never fails."

God sent His Son Jesus, our perfect example of pure and true love. His love can be applied to every aspect of our lives to heal our pain and brokenness. Let us seek out that one person today to show some love. Let loving one another be a choice just as Jesus did for the whole wide world.

Prayer

Dear heavenly Father, thank you for your loving-kindness and unconditional love. Thank you for loving us through our faults and failures. We are ever so grateful to you for a demonstration of real true genuine love. Help me to *love*, as you *love*.

If there be any reason I am tempted not to walk in love, let me ask the question: what about love? This I ask in Jesus's name. Amen!

A Prayer for the Children

D ear Heavenly Father, our Lord and Savior, thank you for the children. We pray for those in school, some of whom are now away from home. They are often confronted with many trials, temptations, and ways to become distracted from who you really are. Lord, let your Holy Spirit keep and guide them. Hide these precious ones under your arm of protection and keep them covered with your blood. Father, grant them the wisdom and knowledge to discern right from wrong and the willpower to resist the wrong. Keep them from being detoured by pressures from their peers and society and all of the unhealthy material and information on the website.

Lord, I ask that you become the face of the book that interests them the most and that they will search you out as diligently as they do their Facebook friends. Give each one of them godly friends and associates. Help them to find freedom in the truth of your word in Proverbs 3:5–6 (NIV):

> Trust in the Lord with all your heart and
> lean not on your own understanding; in all your
> ways acknowledge him, and he will make your
> path straight.

Lord, let them see themselves in the light of your eye as you see them and let them see that they are truly precious in your sight. Open their understanding and increase their learning ability to excel in ways unthinkable.

Lord, help them to never be discouraged or disenchanted when things are not going their way. Have them to know that they may fall down, but you can help them get back up again. Open the floodgate of your love to overflow them with more love than anything or anybody in this world. Let them always look to you, our gracious and merciful Father. Help them to place full confidence in you and to trust you without reservation. This I ask in Jesus's name. Amen.

Prayer of Gratitude

For by him were all things created, that are in heaven
and that are in earth, visible and invisible, whether they
be thrones, or dominions, or principalities, or powers:
all things were created by him, and for him.
—Colossians 1:16 (KJV)

O Lord God, everlasting Father, you are mighty and awesome. Heaven and earth are full of your glory. We adore and exalt you. We praise and magnify your holy and righteous name. Thank you for this world is your creation and you gave us stewardship over your possessions that we may enjoy the benefits. Thank you for your only Son, Jesus, who gave his life that we may live in your presence throughout eternity.

Most gracious and merciful Father, you are the same God today as you were in yesteryears. You've done marvelous things where as we are grateful. We thank you for your ever-lasting arms that the Church has been leaning and depending on for many years. Thank you for every bishop, first family, missionary, parishioner, and visitor that has been a part of this body of believers and was a contributor in the building up of the church. Thank you for our trials that came to make us strong. Thank you for our valleys, which forced us to look up to you. Thank you for our mountain-top experiences, which caused us to praise you.

Lord, as we move forward, let us never forget it was you who brought us this far on the way and that it is not about us but all about you. Lord, help us to be ever grateful and not as the Israelites forgetting how and what you brought us through. We ask that you order our way and steps in your Word. Help us to be good stewards of your possessions. Lord, grant us the will power to love one another as you loved the church, which should make our sharing and caring much easier.

We say to the African Methodist Episcopal Church this day and the Church Universal, "The Lord bless thee and keep thee; the Lord make his face shine upon thee and be gracious unto thee; The Lord lift up his countenance upon thee, and give thee peace" (Numbers 6:24–26 KJV). This we ask in the name of Jesus. Amen.

About the Author

D essie J. Dantzler is a native of Bonita, Louisiana. In 1991, she
moved to California after residing in Chicago, Illinois, for
many years. She is member of Ward African Methodist Episcopal
Church. She is a devoted Christian and dedicated prayer warrior and
is also an active member of the Women's Missionary Society where
she serves as the worship director. In 2006, she traveled to South
Africa with the AME church group on a medical mission in several
rural areas. She served as the AME fifth district missionary prayer
team leader, in which, through that experience, she was motivated to
write devotionals and prayers for the missionary newsletter.

She is a retiree from the medical field after many years of serv-
ing and caring for others as a registered nurse and unit manager. She
has traveled throughout the world extensively, which includes but is
not limited to Jerusalem, Egypt, London, Italy, Spain, New Zealand,
Australia, Greece, and others.

She is a sister, aunt, blended family mother, grandmother,
and great-grandmother. She lives with her husband in Los Angeles,
California.